LIFE SKILLS

Got Career Goals?

Skills to Land Your Dream Job

Louise Spilsbury

Enslow Publishing

101 W. 23rd Street
Suite 240
New York, NY 10011
USA

enslow.com

Published in 2019 by Enslow Publishing, LLC.
101 W. 23rd Street, Suite 240, New York, NY 10011

Cataloging-in-Publication Data

Names: Spilsbury, Louise.
Title: Got career goals? skills to land your dream job / Louise Spilsbury.
Description: New York : Enslow Publishing, 2019. | Series: Life skills | Includes index.
Identifiers: ISBN 9780766099845 (pbk.) | ISBN 9780766099838 (library bound)
Subjects: LCSH: Job hunting--Juvenile literature. | Vocational guidance--Juvenile literature.
Classification: LCC HF5382.7 S65 2019 | DDC 650.14--dc23

Printed in the United States of America

To Our Readers: We have done our best to make sure all website addresses in this book were active and appropriate when we went to press. However, the author and the publisher have no control over and assume no liability for the material available on those websites or on any websites they may link to. Any comments or suggestions can be sent by e-mail to customerservice@enslow.com.

Contents

Chapter 1
Why the Rush?

Why do you need to think about careers now? After all, it will be years before you are working in a full-time job and paying for your own food and house bills! That is true, but it's also a fact that the subjects you choose to take at school now, the effort you put in and the grades you get on tests, and the things you do in your free time can all influence or affect the type of job you may have in the future.

TOUGH MARKETS

The **job market** today is increasingly **competitive**, meaning there are more people going for the same jobs. One reason for this is that most people retire at an older age today than they did in the past, and at the moment the global population is still increasing. With more people looking for work, you need to be able to show why you are better suited to a job than the other applicants. That is why it's never too early to start to thinking about your career. You can start to plan ahead, and maybe seek experience that could help you get into college or land a job one day.

Lots of kids get asked, "What do you want to do when you grow up?" What ideas do you have for your future?

KNOW WHAT WORKS FOR YOU!

The world of work is waiting for you, and planning ahead can be exciting.

Another reason to start thinking about careers when you are young is that no one knows you better than you! Figuring out what interests you, what kind of person you are, what skills you have, and what you would like to learn will help you to know what kind of employment might be best for you. No one is saying you have to choose your career path now, or make a final decision about a job you will do for your whole life. Just think about what direction you would like to be headed in. You can always change your mind later, or change jobs after you start working, but it is still helpful, and fun, to plan ahead!

Dream Jobs

When you sit somewhere quiet, close your eyes, and imagine your dream job, what would it be? Some people say the best way to choose is to think about what you would do if you did not have to work, or were wealthy enough not to worry about how much money you earn. Your choice might not realistically be the best, or even a possible career option. However, it is a good place to start because it makes you ask questions about yourself. This can really help you when it comes to thinking about what job you could do.

It takes years of training to become an airline pilot. Those interested in flying can also get jobs conducting flight-testing, training, and managing and supervising pilot operations.

DREAM BIG

Some dream jobs are a little more "out there." Some kids dream of being an astronaut, and venturing beyond Earth's atmosphere, because they have read about the wonders of space and they have learned about planets and stars. Someone who likes music and singing may envision themselves as the next big pop star, packing venues with their adoring fans. If you play sports, maybe you long to be a famous professional athlete. There is always a chance you could make it big and get a job like this, and no one should squash your dreams. At the same time, be aware that it takes an exceptional amount of luck, **dedication**, and hard work to reach some of these goals.

HAVE A BACK-UP PLAN

While thinking about your dream jobs, you should also think about how you will earn a living. It's a good idea to have a back-up plan if you have a dream job that is difficult to achieve. For example, someone who is a high-school football star and decides to pursue their dream of being a pro player may decide to continue their math studies as well, so they can become an **accountant** if they do not make it in football.

Only around one in 10,000 high school athletes will succeed as a professional athlete, so dream big but have a back-up plan too.

Keeping It Real

Some people's dreams are realistic from an early age. Many children dream of becoming a teacher, possibly because this is a career they see in action every week, and because they enjoy school. They also like the idea of a job that helps others. As people get older, fewer want to be movie stars and astronauts, and more of them want more mainstream careers.

TURNING DREAMS INTO REALITY

One way of turning your dreams into reality is to think of careers within your dream industry. So, for example, if your dream job is to be a movie star, you could consider a different job that involves performing, such as being a **broadcast journalist**. You could study journalism or communications in college, and get a job in a local news or other TV studio. If you hold dreams of traveling the world, why not think about getting a job as a travel guide, **courier**, or flight attendant? These jobs would all give you the chance to travel while you earn a living. These careers are still linked to your dream jobs, but they are more attainable.

In the end, the career you choose is your decision, but it is always a good idea to ask other people for their advice and ideas, too.

There are hundreds of great career options out there that you probably have no idea even exist. Maybe you are interested in medicine, but do not want to be a doctor. What about being a dentist or a dental hygienist? It is only by learning about careers that you will find out about opportunities.

There is a whole world of jobs to explore, from the ones we see people doing, such as dentistry, to those we don't, like medical equipment technician!

Skills for Life

Do not worry if you have no idea what job you would like to do yet. Most people your age have no idea, and if they do, they often change their mind along the way. Reading this book is a good start. You could also ask for advice from people who know you. What ideas do they have, and what have they noticed you are good at?

When adults ask what you want to be when you grow up, they might also ask what school subjects you are good at and enjoy. That is because the subjects you like and are good at can be really useful indicators of what jobs might suit you in the future. It's not as simple as thinking, "I'm good at English, so I should be an English teacher." The skills you need to be good at a subject can lead you in many different directions. That is why it is useful to think now about the skills you have and how they might be suited to a whole variety of jobs.

USING MATH AND SCIENCE SKILLS

If you are good at math, a wide range of jobs is available to you. Workers in almost all professions need math skills. Bankers, accountants, and **engineers** need math skills, but so do meteorologists (weather forecasters) who use math to assess weather data, roller-coaster **designers** who use math to figure out safe angles and slopes, and even chefs who need to calculate ingredients. If you are good at science, you are good at observing and studying the world around you. People who are good at science could become veterinarians, doctors, dentists, nurses, pharmacists, fabric technologists, **geologists**, and more.

Studying math helps you develop skills in logical thinking, problem-solving, and decision-making, which are useful in many jobs.

Food technologists make sure food products are produced safely and legally. They are involved in creating recipes, too.

TAKING TALENTS FURTHER

What if design and technology are your best subjects? You could look at careers in product or **interior design**, woodworking, food technology, or any job that requires creative thinking about designing products and materials that people use. If you are good at English, you could think about working as a journalist, librarian, teacher, editor, bookseller, advertising **copywriter**, or many other careers that require good skills in communicating verbally and in writing. For example, business and marketing managers need to be able to convey information in creative and critical ways.

Home In on Hobbies

Our hobbies and other things we do in our spare time when we are young can also be great indicators of jobs we might turn to later. Think about the hobbies you are good at and enjoy. Could they lead you to a career? Although it can be hard to make a career out of some hobbies, it can be done.

HOBBIES THAT CAN BECOME JOBS

If you are into photography now, you could work as a photographer taking photos of news events, or of the natural world, or of people's special events such as weddings. If you love sports and keeping fit, you could become a personal trainer. A personal trainer is someone who helps individual clients to work out in the gym or at home. Or you could train to become a referee. Nothing is off the table. For example, if you enjoy video games, you could become a tester, designer, or **programmer** of video games in the future. Or you could work in a computer or technology store, helping people to find the right computer system for their needs. There are many jobs that require good skills in the information technology field.

Lots of people like video games, so to succeed in this industry you need to set yourself apart. Maybe try your hand at creating a game of your own!

If you love what you do and you are good at it, you might be able to turn your hobby into a career!

HOBBIES ARE FOR FUN

Of course, the hobbies you choose to do should mostly be just for fun. You should do stuff because you enjoy it, not because it might look good on a job application. But it is also worth remembering that the stuff you do for fun might lead you to a career, and that if you have a definite career in mind, it might be worth taking classes or joining clubs that can give you experience or skills to help you along that path.

Talent Shows

We are all good at different things. If you feel uncertain about where your talents lie, think about what you are good at, not only at school but at home, too. Some talents are easier to spot than others. Almost everyone can see when a student is good at art, or science experiments, while other talents might be harder to pick out immediately. For example, you may be especially kind, thoughtful, and caring. Those valuable qualities can make you suitable for a wide range of jobs. Perhaps you are really creative, with an imagination that can dream up new inventions, or great stories. Make a list of your five best skills and talents. Ask for suggestions from friends and family as well. You may be surprised by what they tell you!

Graphic designers create images and brands for a variety of products, such as websites, books, magazines, posters, computer games, and packaging.

If you want to turn your hobby into a career you will need to work at it.

When you know what you are really good at and love doing, it's a good idea to focus on those talents, and develop them. You could find other people who share your interests, and work on them together. Join a club, or create one if you cannot find one. Take a class, or find a way to use your skills in your community. This will help you to improve, and ensure you devote some time to your skills on a regular basis.

Skills for Life

Hobbies can give you experience and ideas. For example, if you want to work in the movies, take any chances you have now to edit or work on videos. Use a program to edit your sister's birthday party video, or work on your uncle's wedding video. You could make your own short film or music video. It's a great thing to do with friends. You could write a script and get friends to act in it, or ask friends who have a band if you can film one of their rehearsals or shows. By doing these things, you will discover if you really enjoy this kind of work, and if you can imagine yourself doing it as a career.

Chapter 3
All About You

Work is not the only thing that affects how happy we are, but you will spend a big chunk of your adult life doing it, so it makes sense to choose a career that suits you and your personality. Work that suits the kind of person you are is much more likely to keep you interested and happy. So, before you start researching careers, spend some time thinking about your personal interests, skills, and values, and what **motivates** you as a person.

If you enjoy helping people and are motivated by improving their lives, caregiving work might be a good career area for you.

ARE YOU IN OR OUT?

One simple question to ask yourself is whether you are an outdoors type or an indoors type. Even if you like being outside some of the time, to ride your bike or swim in a pool, would you be content if you were indoors for your working day? Are you happy to be inside working on a school project, or a hobby? Do you like working with ideas, numbers, computers, or words? Do you find that the thought of being outdoors all day is not appealing? If that is the case, you are probably more suited to some kind of office, store, or service job. There are hundreds of jobs where people work indoors. You could work caring for children or the elderly, or be a museum or art gallery **curator**. You could be an accountant, **architect**, chef, web developer, manicurist or beautician, teacher, editor, designer, retail assistant, nurse, or receptionist. The list is huge!

If you prefer to be outside, one job you could consider is gardening.

TAKE IT OUTSIDE!

What if you prefer working with your hands, and being outdoors all day? There are plenty of jobs that allow people to make the countryside, oceans, deserts, or wilderness their place of work. For example, landscape architects design green spaces such as parks. Land surveyors collect and analyze data to map the land for construction projects, like new housing estates. If you are an outdoors type, becoming a firefighter, gardener, **marine biologist**, farmer, forest ranger, lifeguard, ski instructor, or adventure tour guide are just a few more of your options.

Team Player or Flying Solo?

In most jobs, it is important to be able to get along well with other people. Some people really like to be part of a team, where they can share ideas and learn from other people's strengths. Such people are usually good at **negotiating** and **compromising**. There are also many jobs for people who work best alone, or alongside others but not directly with them. These are the kind of people who usually prefer to speak with one or two people at a time, rather than a big group, and need more personal space. Of course, there are also lots of jobs that allow you to work alone for some of the time, and as part of a team the rest of the time!

Experiencing working in a team is good for everyone.

TEAMWORK

Being someone who can work well as part of a team is vital for many jobs. The most obvious example is athletes on a sports team. Having a bunch of talented players does not guarantee success for the team. A team that works hard and has great teamwork can beat a group of more talented players that is not working well as a team. Teamwork is not just needed on the sports field. It is necessary in a whole range of jobs. Soldiers, salespeople, nurses, doctors, restaurant staff, government workers, construction workers, firefighters, and many other workers must have good teamwork skills.

Some people prefer jobs or tasks that require them to spend more time alone rather than working in teams.

GOING IT ALONE

Some people prefer to work alone, because they like to rely on their own efforts, and stay in control of their working life. They might prefer the kind of job that allows them to work independently, and focus without distraction from others around them. Some careers suited to people who prefer to work alone include fine art, graphic design, computer animation or programming, web development, interior design, and video-game development. People who work alone in research labs may work mostly on their own, though they are usually part of a wider team in the same department or building.

Many of the social skills people have cannot be tested with exams, but they are incredibly important for a whole variety of jobs. For example, the ability to communicate quickly and efficiently is very important for a team of firefighters. Firefighters have radios fitted to their helmets so they can keep in contact with each other at all times, warning each other of danger, helping to find casualties, and instructing where and when their equipment is needed. Being able to think and communicate quickly in this situation can mean the difference between life and death.

*Being able to work as part of a team is a great **transferable skill** and is essential as a firefighter.*

WHAT ARE TRANSFERABLE SKILLS?

Communication skills are one kind of transferable skill. Transferable skills are abilities that are relevant and helpful across different areas of life, including socially, at school, and in all sorts of different jobs. These are skills like problem-solving, which is being able to think things through in a logical or creative way to figure out the most important issues and how to address them. Some people are also more flexible, or able to adapt, than others, so they are better at changing and adapting to new situations. Another transferable skill is motivation: some people have a lot of energy and enthusiasm to bring to projects, which can encourage others to achieve, too. Other people have good **initiative**, meaning they can spot opportunities and set and achieve goals, or they may have good **interpersonal** skills, meaning they relate well to other people.

SCHEDULE

‹ ›

DAY   WEEK   **MONTH**

30	31	1	2	3	4	5
				OFFICE OUTING		
6	7	8	9	10	11	12
		ANNUAL LEAVE				
13	14	15	16	17	18	19
				MEETING WITH MR.JONES		OLC'53 REUNION
20	21	22	23	24	25	26
			CUSTOMER VISIT			
27	28	29	30	1	2	3
DINNER WITH FAMILY			MONTHLY REPORT			

If you are good at problem-solving and organizing things, you will find these are skills you can use in a variety of jobs.

Skills for Life

Qualifications are not the only key to success. Many employers also seek out people who have transferable skills, such as leadership abilities and interpersonal skills. Many jobs require transferable skills such as being a good organizer, or being able to take the initiative in a situation. Think about the transferable skills you have. Are you good at organizing stuff, or doing research? Are you a natural leader, or are you great at getting along with people?

Chapter 4
Check It Out!

Once you have identified your particular interests, skills, and talents, you need to find out about what jobs are out there that could be right for you. When you have found some jobs you like the sound of, you can start to learn about them.

Researching careers is important. The more you find out about jobs, the better placed you will be to make decisions about which career path to follow.

DO YOUR HOMEWORK

There are many books and websites devoted to this subject. Government and other websites may divide the jobs by subject. So, for example, if you are good at science or art, you can search under these subjects to find a list of the jobs you could do. Other sites list the careers alphabetically. Some websites include videos explaining what people do in this job, and even interviews with workers who describe what they do and why they like it. This kind of detailed information can really help you to learn about what jobs are out there, and what they are really like. Many websites also have quizzes, or other interactive tools that can help you match your skills with future career options.

NEW JOBS

Another reason for doing your research is because the job market is always changing. There are even totally new jobs developing in some industries. In a world threatened by climate change, there are many new jobs in green and **renewable energy**. For example, there are new jobs testing water quality, designing and producing new cars that run on electricity rather than gasoline, recycling, doing construction work using green techniques such as installing solar panels or environmentally friendly heating systems, or building whole houses out of recycled materials. If you read the news, and keep on top of what's going on in the world, you will also learn about the new kinds of jobs that may be available to you in the future.

Research can help you discover the new kinds of jobs that are springing up all the time, such as in the renewable energy industry.

Find Out More

There are other ways of finding out more about possible careers. When you are considering any career option, remember to ask about the possible advantages and disadvantages of working in that job. Also, ask if there is anything you can do now to help you in achieving your goals.

Career fairs provide a great chance for people to ask lots of questions, to discover as much as they can about a variety of different employers.

CAREER FAIRS

A career fair is an event where people can meet with employers to find out about different jobs and businesses where they might like to work. Most career fairs are designed for adults, but some provide an opportunity for young people to meet employers. You could even ask your school if they, maybe jointly with other local schools, could organize a career fair like this. Most local businesses, and even those from farther away, would be happy to send people over for a day to a fair like this to show people what they do and what job opportunities they have available.

EXTRA INFORMATION

While exploring your options, you might want to take time to consider other things a job or career can provide. For example, where would you have to travel to for the type of job you are interested in? Is there work near your home and family, or do you want to move away? Would you prefer to live in a town, or out in the countryside? What about salary? Which is more important to you: job satisfaction or a high salary? Are you looking for a job with prospects for traveling abroad? Are you ambitious, and if so, would you like to be in an industry or business where you work extra hard to get regular promotions to more senior positions in the company? Alternatively, is it more important to you to have a nine-to-five job, so you can spend time outside regular working hours doing other things? These are all important things to consider, because we spend many years working.

Some jobs don't have set hours and can take you anywhere. Finding out this kind of information early on can be really helpful.

See How It Fits

Have you ever gone with your mom or dad to a "take your children to work" day? Did you make the most of your day? Your parents' jobs might not be right for you, but seeing any workplace is a great chance to learn. Sit down with them the night before you go, ask them about their work, and discuss what you would like to get out of the day. For example, if they work in a big company, there may be a department you are interested in that they could show you around. Some kids go along to their aunt or uncle's workplace instead, if that family member does a job they are more interested in.

Before you visit a place of work with a member of your family, jot down ideas about what you'd like to learn or which jobs or departments you'd like to find out more about.

Skills for Life

While researching a job online or in real life, ask yourself these questions:

- How does the job match with my skills, interests, and values?
- What are the advantages and disadvantages of each job?
- Is there anything that could help or hinder me in getting that job?

Shadowing someone while they perform their job is a perfect chance to learn about a career.

SHADOWING

Essentially what you are doing on a day when you go with a parent or other relative to work for a day is job shadowing. Job shadowing is when you follow someone around in their workplace and watch them doing a job you might like to do. Shadowing is a great way to get a sense of what it is truly like working at that job. Many adults, including students and recent **graduates**, do this when they are considering different job options. Try to find opportunities to shadow different jobs, perhaps through your family members or their friends. When you are shadowing for a day, if you get the chance, politely ask questions about both the good and the bad aspects of their job.

Chapter 5
A Plan of Action

Once you know what type of job interests you, it is time to make a plan of action. First, you need to find out what qualifications, experience, or skills will help you reach your goal, and how you can achieve these things. It can help to write down a plan of action. What do you need to know? Where can you find that information? Who can help? Write down the things you need to do and then follow that plan. Being informed is important, and it really helps to have a plan to follow so you do not keep putting off the research.

Teachers and guidance counselors can help you find the information you need about your job choices.

WHAT SKILLS DO I NEED?

There are lots of ways to find out more about the skills and qualifications you need for a job. You can research careers online on websites that give all sorts of information about different jobs, including salaries and lists of the school grades or experience required. There are also pages where individuals talk about doing their jobs, and how they got them. You could also talk to your teachers. If they do not know the answers, they will be able to show you where to find the information you need. Most schools also have guidance counselors who are trained to help students with this type of information.

THE JOB MARKET

It is also worth doing some research into how your options fit with the current job market. For example, in the United States the electronics and software industries are growing, with demand for graduates exceeding supply. Other areas where there has been an increase in the number of jobs available are healthcare, engineering, education, and finance. If you follow the news, you will know where there are more job options, and this could improve your chances of getting a job after you have gained your qualifications or completed your training.

Keep on top of the news and what is going on in the world. Then you'll know what career areas are expanding, and therefore the areas in which you are best placed to find a job.

The Apprentice

Many people learn a trade, or how to do a job, by becoming an **apprentice**. Apprenticeships are a win-win, both for the employers who run the programs and for the trainee workers who do the apprenticeships. Employers get a chance to find good workers for the future, and train them in the way they want the job to be done. Workers get to learn a trade, while earning some money at the same time. Apprenticeships take one to four years to complete, depending on the type of job and its level. You can start looking for apprenticeships, and even apply for one, while you are still at school.

Being an apprentice engineer gives you the chance to learn about the profession from highly experienced people.

HOW APPRENTICESHIPS WORK

The idea behind apprenticeship is not new. It has been around for hundreds of years. Apprenticeship has been the main way in which a craft or trade has been passed on from one generation to another. In order to become a skilled worker in many trades, particularly in the building and construction industry, people usually start off in a training program, where they work alongside an experienced tradesman. By working for and alongside the skilled, older worker, an apprentice learns all the skills needed to do the job well.

BENEFITS OF BEING AN APPRENTICE

There are many benefits of apprenticeships. Apprentices often receive some academic study combined with their on-the-job training. This educational study can also give you nationally recognized qualifications. In some apprenticeships, you can earn as much as 50 percent of what you will be earning after you are trained while you learn on the job. Another major benefit is that if the company you train with likes you, they will likely employ you fully after you have successfully completed the apprenticeship.

Many hairdressers and stylists learned their skills through apprenticeships.

Making the Grade

Some jobs need qualifications, such as a college or university degree. College and university programs begin after high school, when a student is seventeen or eighteen years old, or older. A two-year college offers an associate's degree, as well as certificates. A four-year college or university offers a bachelor's degree. Programs that offer these degrees are called undergraduate schools.

Studying for a degree can be hard work but most people agree it is well worth it.

DIFFERENT KINDS OF DEGREES

A university has at least one college where students receive a bachelor's degree. The other schools in a university are graduate or postgraduate schools, where students receive advanced degrees. So, at a university you can earn both a bachelor's degree and a graduate degree, such as a master's (M.A.) and a doctorate (Ph.D.). Some careers will require not only a degree but also other educational qualifications or experience. For example, it typically requires a total of seven years to qualify as a lawyer, including four years of undergraduate coursework to gain a bachelor's degree, and three years of law school to become a Juris Doctor (J.D.).

Skills for Life

There are many routes to getting a job, and you can choose to earn a degree even if you are not totally sure of the career you want to do. Some people choose to earn a degree that is **vocational**, and some graduate jobs require you to have studied a particular subject, or range of subjects, designed to equip you for that career. For example, if you want to be a doctor you will need to earn a degree in medicine, and to do that you need to study science subjects in school. Other careers are open to graduates from any subject. For example, there are not many careers that specifically demand an arts degree, such as English or history, but there are still many roles for which arts graduates are eligible.

There are some careers, such as being a lawyer, that you can only do if you have the relevant degree.

Chapter 6

Make It Happen

So, you might know what sort of career you are interested in, and you know what kind of qualifications and experience you need to get it. Now you just have to put your head down and do your best in school. Make the most of your free time, also, to help you achieve those aims. Most things that are worth having require time and effort, and you can make this happen.

GETTING THE BEST OUT OF SCHOOL

One way to do the best you can in school is to make an effort to listen and ask questions. Do not be embarrassed to raise your hand and ask a teacher to explain something again. Chances are, some of your classmates didn't quite get it, either. Reading over the tricky stuff when you get home might also help you understand it better. Don't be hard on yourself if you find something difficult. Focus on the positives, and on what you can do. It is equally important to stick to things. Remind yourself you need those grades to achieve your goal, and although it might be tempting to turn on the TV and leave the schoolwork for another day, you will enjoy your time relaxing more if you get your work finished first.

It is important to keep up with your homework. Falling behind will just make homework harder.

GETTING THROUGH TESTS

Everyone works in different ways, and understanding the way you learn best will help you to do better in school. For example, some people learn well when they listen to music, or if someone else tests them on practice questions. Others prefer to work alone, in silence. Find what works best for you, and make it happen. If you respond well to working on the computer, download programs you can work through. If you study and remember things better if they are presented visually, make yourself pictures and diagrams of the stuff you need to learn.

Extra, Extra!

Extracurricular means the things you do that fall outside of the regular school curriculum, or program of courses and subjects. These extra things that you do after school, at lunch, or on weekends might include sports, or music, or painting. As well as obtaining the qualifications and grades you need to get ahead, doing some carefully chosen extracurricular activities can help you succeed with some career choices. They can increase your chances of being noticed when you apply for your dream job, because they show you have had a long-term interest in that field.

The activities you do that take place outside of the classroom can help you get a job.

TAKE IT A STEP FURTHER

Doing extracurricular activities gives you experience, and it also proves to others that you have spent time nurturing your hobby or talent. For example, imagine you want to be a singer. It does not matter if you sing for hours every day, if you only sing around the house or in the shower. Why not join a community singing group, or participate in summer musical theater? You will gain a lot of experience, learn new things about music and theater, and you will also have theater programs and photographs to prove to colleges and companies that you have been working on developing your skills from a young age.

When you are competing against another person for a job, being able to prove you did extracurricular activities might cinch the deal in your favor!

HOW IT HELPS

Research shows that most businesses think extracurricular activities make job-seeking young people stand out from the crowd. People who have extracurricular experience often progress more quickly in their careers, too. This is because doing extra classes, clubs, or sports helps participants to develop transferable skills, such as leadership and communication. These are skills that are highly valued in a whole variety of jobs. So, instead of just heading home after school, consider staying for an after-school club or going to an extra class or two.

Work Experience

Work experience is the ideal way to discover how you would spend your time on a typical day in a job. Having work experience also impresses potential employers. The other great thing about work experience is that it gives you a chance to try out different jobs, so you can change direction if necessary. Learning what you do not want to do is just as important as figuring out what you do want to do!

Some young people build a career from their part-time job.

PART-TIME AND SUMMER JOBS

Although you should not take on a part-time job that would interfere with your ability to do your schoolwork, a part-time job can give you work experience and help you to develop useful skills, such as teamwork and timekeeping. It can also give you a written reference, or recommendation, from your part-time employer. This can be really helpful when you apply for jobs and courses in the future. Part-time jobs are usually available in a number of places, including stores, restaurants, cafes or fast food outlets, call centers, and hair salons. You could also think about getting a job during your summer vacation, to gain direct or transferable skills to help you find employment. For example, you could work at theme parks, hotels, beach clubs, or ranches.

VOLUNTEERING

Volunteering is when you work without being paid, often for an organization that is working for a good cause. For example, you could volunteer to help clean a local beach, or work in a thrift store. You could help family members or friends deliver meals to the homebound, plant flowers at a local park, or spend time helping people with disabilities. It is always worth asking a charity you are interested in if they offer opportunities for children or families to get involved. Another idea is to offer to help a teacher or coach you know to run their extracurricular classes, or activities for younger children. Make use of any contacts you have.

Volunteering improves your skills and experience, and can also help you stand out from the crowd. Plus, it feels good to do something worthwhile.

Make the Most of It

To get the most out of any work experience, volunteer or part-time, try to treat it like a real job. That means being punctual, turning up on time every day. You should dress appropriately in something clean, to show you care. Make an effort every time you work. Be polite and ask questions. If you don't know how to do something, don't just wing it. Ask someone to show you, and pay attention so that you can do it alone next time. If you finish one task, don't hang around until someone notices. Be enthusiastic and ask for another job. People will love your enthusiasm, and you will get more experience!

Make the most of any work experience you get.

IMPRESSING AT INTERVIEWS

Even part-time jobs or volunteer work may require you to have an interview, to find out if you are suitable for the role. It is natural to feel a little nervous about interviews, but you can make the best of them by being prepared. Do your research about what the job will involve, and think of practical examples, such as from school projects or volunteering activities, which demonstrate you have these skills. If employers ask you why you have applied for the position, answer with enthusiasm about the role and an interest in the company.

Skills for Life

If you have to do an interview, you could role-play with a family member or friend before you go. Think about how best to answer a few practice interview questions, such as:

- Why have you applied for this role?
- What relevant skills and experience do you have?
- How is your personality suited to this job?
- What do you know about the company?
- What are your biggest strengths and your greatest weaknesses?

Preparing for an interview in advance and perhaps role-playing it with a friend will help you perform well in an interview.

Make a Note of It

When an art student applies for college, or wants to show their work to a studio or potential employer, they take along a portfolio. This is a big folder containing samples of all their best work. Having a portfolio like this is especially important for visual arts and arts majors, but it can be useful for all students. Keeping a record of all the things you do that could be relevant to a career you want to do in the future is a great idea. You may not need to show it all to a potential employer, but records like this will help you to remember what you have done. That will be really useful when you come to write your **resume**.

A portfolio is a collection of artwork, documents, letters, or other proof of your talent or experience.

BUILDING A RESUME

A resume is a page or two of text in which people list their skills, interests, education, and achievements. It is also one of the best ways of advertising yourself to an employer. It gives you the chance to show them that you are qualified, skilled, and ready for work, and to explain what sets you apart from the rest. So, when you do something interesting or worthwhile, keep a record of it so you can use it to build a great resume later. This could include materials from events and activities you helped organize. It could be a certificate from a training course or a music exam, or a letter from an employer at a company where you volunteered, thanking you for your time and effort.

When you achieve something special, like passing an exam or performing in a concert, write it on your resume.

MAKING NOTES

As well as certificates, letters, and programs, keep notes about what you did, and what each experience taught you. For example, did a volunteer job help you to develop any skills that might be useful in a future job? Did a club you joined give you experience of working on a team? Did helping younger children teach you to give instructions well, or help you to develop leadership skills?

You Can Do It!

Thinking about potential careers should be fun and empowering. Having an idea of what sort of job you might like in the future can inspire you to make the most of your school life now, and encourage you to try out extracurricular activities you may not have thought of before. Of course, you may choose a career today that feels right for you now, but change your mind later. Even if you end up following a different career path later, thinking now about what you want to do for your working life is still worthwhile. Trying different activities will make you a happier, more interesting person, and will open doors to new friendships and opportunities. You will gain skills, and build a resume that could lead you in new directions. It will also build your confidence, and that will help you in whatever career path you follow.

Taking charge of your life and your possible future feels good.

Skills for Life

Follow these steps to plan for your career.

- Think about what school subjects you are good at.

- List the hobbies you have and what else you enjoy doing.

- Figure out what kind of personality you have, and what your values and interests are.

- Research jobs that reflect your talents, interests, and personality.

- Find out what qualifications and experience you need to be able to do the jobs that appeal to you.

- Work hard at school to get the grades you need.

- Take extra classes, or join clubs, to improve your talents and skills.

- Get some work experience or part-time work linked to your chosen career.

- Keep a record of all you do that might be relevant to those career choices.

- Finally, you will be able to go out there and get a job!

Work hard at school and you might land your dream job.

accountant A person whose job is to check the financial records (or accounts) of individuals or businesses.

apprentice A person who is learning to do a trade or job, often while also studying part-time.

architect A person who designs buildings and in many cases also supervises their construction.

broadcast journalist A person who writes for newspapers, magazines, or TV, or prepares news to be broadcast.

competitive Having a strong desire to compete or to succeed.

compromising Settling a dispute or solving a problem by giving up some of the things you want.

copywriter A person who writes the words of advertisements or publicity materials.

courier A person employed to guide and assist a group of tourists.

curator A person who is in charge of the objects in a museum or gallery.

dedication The quality of being wholly committed to something. For example, a dedicated marathon runner trains every day.

designers People who design things. Graphic designers combine text and pictures in advertisements, magazines, websites, or books.

engineers People who design, build, or maintain engines, machines, or structures.

geologists Scientists who study the Earth and the processes that shape it.

graduates People who have successfully completed a course of study or training.

initiative The ability to get things going, have new ideas, or start a new project.

interior design The design and decoration inside buildings.

interpersonal Relating to relationships or communication between people.

job market The jobs that are available for workers.

marine biologist A scientist who studies things that live in the oceans and seas.

motivates Gives someone a reason or the enthusiasm to do something.

negotiating Dealing or bargaining with other people.

programmer Someone who writes computer programs.

renewable energy Energy from a source that is not depleted when used, such as wind, water, or the sun.

resume A brief description of a person's education, qualifications, previous occupations, and interests, typically sent with a job application.

transferable skill A skill that is useful across different areas of life, socially, at school, and in all sorts of different jobs.

vocational Teaching the skills you need for a particular job.

Further Reading

BOOKS

Beddell, J.M. *So, You Want to Work with Animals?* New York: Aladdin/Beyond Words, 2017.

Higgins, Melissa. *Build Your Business.* North Mankato, MN: Capstone Press, 2017.

Higgins, M.G. & P.J. Gray. *Finding a Job/ Dream Jobs*. Costa Mesa, CA: Saddleback Educational Publishing, 2017.

Mitchell, P.P. *US Armed Forces*. New York: Gareth Stevens Publishers, 2017.

Reeve, Diane Lindsay. *World of Work*. North Mankato, MN: Bright Futures Press, Cherry Lake Publishing, 2017.

Stoltman, Joan. *Gareth Guides to an Extraordinary Life*. New York: Gareth Stevens Publishers, 2017.

WEBSITES

CareerOneStop
www.careeronestop.org/ExploreCareers/
explore-careers.aspx
This is a great place to explore different careers and the qualifications you need for each one.

Bureau of Labor Statistics
https://www.bls.gov/k12/
This website helps high-school kids choose careers.

Kids.gov
kids.usa.gov/teens/jobs/a-z-list/index.shtml
There is an A-Z list of jobs here, taking you to videos and much more information.

Index